Ideas for a Fun and Imaginative Backyard

Ideas for a Fun and Imaginative Backyard

"How Different Would Your Life Be Today If You'd Been Given The Skill To Actually Achieve Goals...?"

Give Your Kids That Gift Today!

The First Book EVER To Explain Goal Setting And the Law Of Attraction in Terms Your Children Will Understand!

'Go for Your Goals - Goal Setting and Visualization for Kids'
Package of 3 Downloadable E-Books

Click Here to Order

"Finally, An Internet Monitoring Software That Records Everything Your Child Does When They Go Online"

As a parent, you have to ask yourself: "Is my child safe when they're online?" Don't bet on it.

With an estimated One MILLION pedophiles online, you need Parental controls to protect your children from child molesters and sexual predators.

WHAT ARE YOUR CHILDREN DOING ONLINE? Use this Internet Monitoring Software and you'll never need to worry.!

Who's Taking To Your Children When They Go Online?

What are your kids doing online?

The An All-In-One Suite of Parental Controls & Internet Monitoring Tools:

Only **PC Tattletale** offers a complete **Internet Monitoring and Parental Control Software solution**, that's unmatched in the industry.

See for yourself how powerful our features are and what they can do for you:

 Monitors MySpace.Com

 Password Capture and Keystroke Recording

 Chat Recorder

 Screen Shot Recording

 Email Monitoring & Reporting

 Web Site History Monitor

 PC Software Monitoring

 URL Specific Web Filtering

 Total Stealth Operation

PC Tattletale Parental control software contains all the **PC monitoring tools** you'll need to keep your child safe - in a single easy to use software suite!

You might be shocked

Click Here

To Find Out

Ideas for a Fun and Imaginative Backyard

Contents

Backyard Activities for the Home Improvement Lover

When we think of backyard activities, sports often come to mind. While sports are a great way to spend your time outdoors, they are not all that backyard activities include. In fact, while you may not necessarily think so, backyard activities also involve the completion of projects. If you are a home improvement lover, it is quite possible that your next backyard activity could involve the building or the remodeling of a structure.

In the United States, backyards are filled with millions of different things. Many homeowners have pools, barns, work sheds, or garages. If you already have these items inside your yard, you may want to think about remodeling them. Remodeling projects are ideal for those who wish to update or expand their backyard structures. Summer is the perfect time to complete many remodeling projects, especially those that are outside.

While many homeowners make the decision to remodel, there are others that choose to build. If you don't have a barn, garage, or work shed, but you would like to have one, now would be the perfect time to start construction. In most areas of the United States, summer has the prefect weather conditions for many backyard projects.

The first step in building or remodeling a backyard structure is to develop a plan. If you already know what you would like to build and how you would like to build it, you are well on your way to a completed project. However, if you are unsure what you would like to build or how to build it, you may want to think about doing a little bit of research before you start your next home improvement project.

Perhaps, the easiest way to get ideas or directions on how to build a garage, work shed, or barn is to visit your local library or book store. In these locations, you should be able to find a number of books that will not only offer you suggestions, but give you directions on how to get started. Libraries are nice; however, you will only be able to keep the materials for a short period of time. If you are interested in saving your resource guides for another project, you may want to consider purchasing your own books.

Once you have decided on a structural design, you will need to obtain the necessary building supplies. The supplies that you need will all depend on what you are building or remodeling. Despite the fact that different projects will require different supplies, there are some supplies that are common among all backyard building or remodeling projects. These supplies may include wood, metal, saws, and many other common household tools.

As previously mentioned, summer is ideal for most construction projects. Even though the weather will most likely be cooperative, it may still be a good idea to check your local weather forecast. If you are doing a project that requires perfect weather, such as roofing or painting, you will want to plan your project around the projected weather forecast. With projects that require more than one days worth of work, you may want to wait until the weather forecast predicts steady weather. This will prevent you from having to stop your building or remodeling and then startup again later.

Although building and remodeling projects are great backyard activities, not everyone is able to do them. If you are inexperienced in construction, you may find it difficult or impossible to do the work yourself. If this is the case, professional assistance may be just what you need. Completing your own home improvement projects will save you money, but only if you know what you are doing. Poor building or remodeling jobs may not only need additional, costly repairs, but they may also be unsafe.

With something as large and important as most home improvement projects, you are advised against taking any unnecessary chances or risks. Whether you make the decision to perform your own home improvement project or sit back and watch a professional do it, you will still be outside, enjoying everything that your backyard and the beautiful weather has to offer.

Gardening: A Fun and Creative Backyard Project

When summer rolls around, many individuals enjoy spending time in their backyard. When it comes to summer, many individuals associate backyards with picnics, barbeques, swimming, and outdoor sports. While all of these activities are nice, there are not the only things that you can do in your backyard. In fact, there are a number of other popular backyard activities that you may never have given much thought to. One of those activities involves growing a garden.

When it comes to gardening, there are many individuals who wonder why they should even bother. Growing a garden may take a lot of time and hard work; however, there are a number of benefits to gardening. To determine if growing a garden would be the perfect backyard activity for you, you are advised to fully examine these benefits. After that examination, you should be able to decide whether or not gardening is an activity that you would enjoy.

One of the many benefits of gardening is that you can design your garden however you want. There are a large number of individuals that choose to grow flowers, plants, or vegetables; however, you do not have to choose just one. If you desire, you could have your garden be a collection of plants, flowers, and vegetables.

You may also find that the type of garden you choose will have a number of benefits. For instance, plant and flower gardens are often beautiful. If you choose to grow plants or flowers, you may find that they help to improve the appearance of your backyard. Vegetable gardens are a great way to save money on food. Many vegetable gardens are composed of potatoes, carrots, tomatoes, and beets. If you are able to successfully grow these foods, you and your family could enjoy them as a tasty treat or part of a meal.

Perhaps, the greatest benefit of gardening is the relaxation. Although garden requires a fairly large amount of work, there are many who feel as if it really isn't work. In fact, there are many gardeners who say that gardening is as great way to relax. This is because you can work at your own pace. In addition to being relaxing, a garden will be your own creation. If are able to successfully grow a garden, you may be pleased with the results and proud of yourself, as you should be.

If you plan on using your garden as a source of relaxation, it is possible that you may prefer gardening by yourself. Even though you may enjoy gardening by yourself, you may also find benefits to including your family in the process, especially if you have young children. There are many children who enjoy helping their parents in the garden. If your child would like to offer you assistance, you could purchase them their own supplies. Most online retailers, toy stores, and department stores carry a selection of age appropriate gardening accessories.

In addition to purchasing gardening accessories for your child, if they are interested in gardening with you, you will have to purchase your own. Gardening supplies include a wide variety of different items. These items, such as hoes, weeding forks, shovels, and knee pads, can be purchased from most retail stores. You may find that a number of these supplies are available for an affordable price.

With the ability to create your own unique garden, improve the appearance of your backyard, grow your own food, and purchase gardening accessories for an affordable price, you are encouraged to at least consider this popular backyard activity. You may find that it is perfect way to spend your summer.

Must Have Accessories For Your Next Gardening Project

If you enjoy gardening, you are not alone. Each year, millions of Americans grow a garden. If you are interested in becoming one of those individuals, you may need to purchase some supplies. These gardening accessories may not only make gardening easier, but they may also help to produce better results.

When it comes to gardening accessories, there are a number of different items that are included. To start a garden and maintain it, it is likely that you will need gardening supplies. To grow plants or food, you will need to have seeds. To help your seeds flourish, you may want to have plant food and other feeding supplies. The gardening tools and supplies that you need will all depend on what type of garden you are interested in developing. Despite the difference in supplies, there are many common accessories that you may wish to have.

The first step in starting a garden is to pick a space. Since your plants, flowers, or food will need sunlight, you will want to select an area that receives an adequate amount of it. This area can either be large or small, depending on the size of your garden. You may also want to make sure that this area is not in the way of your other activities. Developing your garden in a fairly secluded area will help to reduce the risk of destruction.

To get started, you will need to have a number of important gardening tools. These tools should be used to dig a hole for your seeds and to create a smooth ground surface. Popular gardening tools include, but should not be limited to, weeding forks, surface rakes, shovels, and hoes. If you do not already have these tools, you will need to purchase them. Most of these garden tools, along with other gardening accessories, can be purchased online or from most department stores or home improvement stores.

Once you have created a safe gardening area, you will then need to start planting your seeds. Your seeds will all depend on which type of garden you plan on having. Many gardeners choose to have a flower garden, plant garden, or a vegetable garden. It addition to having one or the other, you may also want to incorporate plants, vegetables and flowers all into one. You can easily obtain seeds by visiting your local home improvement store, garden store, or department store. For hard to find seeds, you may need to resort to online shopping.

Depending on the type of flowers, plants, or vegetables you planted, you should begin to see results in a few weeks. Plant food and special soil may help to increase the appearance of your garden. While most gardeners prefer to use plant food, it is optional. In some cases, you may find that your plants, flowers, or vegetables will grow just as well on their own. Plant food and premixed food soils can be purchased for an affordable price at most retail stores.

Gardening is a backyard activity that many enjoy themselves. If you are a parent, you may also want to include your child. Depending on their age, age appropriate gardening tools can be purchased. These tools are similar to most traditional tools, but they tend to be safer. In fact, most play gardening tools are made of plastic and have dull edges. To purchase these gardening supplies for your child, you will want to visit your local retail store or shop online.

Must Have Accessories For All Backyard Activities

Backyard activities, there are literally an unlimited number of them. Whether you enjoy the water, playing sports, or just relaxing, there is likely at least one backyard activity that will appeal to you or to your family. While backyard activities are nice, there are many that require the purchase of equipment or additional accessories. If you are interested in participating in a popular backyard activity, you may want to first examine the equipment or supplies that you may need.

One popular backyard activity that many enjoy may not really even be considered an activity. When relaxing, many individuals are taking a small break. However, in addition to using relaxation as a break from many other activities, there are others who use it just for the purpose of taking in a piece environment. Many enjoy just sitting outside alone, reading a book, doing homework, or working on other projects. While it nice to relax outside, you will need to have the proper equipment. This equipment often includes patio or lawn furniture.

While patio and lawn furniture is most commonly used for relaxation, it is also important for other activities, such as eating or outdoor crafts. In fact, whether you regularly participate in backyard activities or not, it may be a good idea to have patio furniture on hand. If you do not already have lawn furniture, you may want to start looking for some. You can easily find a selection of patio sets or picnic tables online or at most retail stores. In addition to patio furniture, you may also want to bring a small pillow or blanket outside.

Depending on the amount of time you plan on staying in your backyard, you may also want to bring out a few snacks and drinks. Whenever you are outdoors, especially during the summer, it is important that you pick your drinks and snacks wisely. During the hot weather, you are advised to stay away from caffeinated beverages or sugary dinks. Instead of a sports drinks or soda, water may be a safer and healthier alternative. As with your drinks, you may also want to avoid snacks that are high in sugar.

Aside from lawn furniture and snacks, most of the other equipment and accessories you will need will depend on what you are doing. For instance, if you are planning on swimming, you will want to look into purchasing pool accessories and pool supplies. Depending on the type of pool you have, these supplies may include, but should not be limited to, pool toys, pool furniture, lifesaving devices, pool fixtures, and pool cleaning supplies. For more information on the accessories and supplies available for pools, you may want to visit the website of an online pool retailer or your local pool supply store.

Even if you are unable to have a pool, you can still enjoy a number of different backyard water activities. Many individuals, especially teenagers, enjoy playing with water balloons or water guns. For a more relaxed water activity, you may want to look into purchasing a water sprinkler. Water sprinklers are a nice alternative to swimming pools. In addition to purchasing water guns, water balloons, or a sprinkler, you may also need to purchase a garden hose. Garden hoses are available for sale at most retail stores, including hardware stores, sports stores, and traditional department stores.

Outdoor sports games, in addition to swimming and other water activities, are also enjoyed by many. If you or your family is interested in playing backyard sports, you may need to purchase some sports equipment. The equipment that you need to have will all depend on which specific games you are planning on playing. For instance, if you are interested in playing volleyball, you will need to purchase a volleyball and a volleyball net. In addition to volleyball, other popular backyard sports games include baseball, softball, soccer, and kickball.

Whether you and your family decide to participate in one of the above mentioned backyard activities or another, it is important that you have the needed supplies and equipment. A baseball game just isn't the same without a glove; in fact, it may even make the sport dangerous. That is why it is important that you know what accessories are needed to make your next backyard outing safe and enjoyable.

Great Food For Your Next Backyard Adventure

Millions of individuals and families retreat to their backyards. While backyards are nice all throughout the year, they are even better in the summertime. To make the most out of your next backyard adventure, you are encouraged to think about what foods, if any, you will have on hand.

When most individuals think of backyards and food, a backyard barbeque often comes to mind. If you and your family are interested in having a backyard barbeque, you will have to decide on the foods in which you would like to cook. If you have a large family or a few picky eaters, you may want to ask your children for suggestions. Suggestions will help to make sure that you have food that everyone will enjoy.

While many families have their own backyard barbeques, there are others who decide to turn their barbeque into a party. If you are interested in having a backyard barbeque party, you may have to purchase a large amount of meat. Whether you are cooking for your family or a large group of people, it may be a good idea to purchase your meats in bulk. Most supermarkets, in the United States, charge less for items purchased in large quantities. If you if you are unable to use all of the meat that you purchased, you should be able to use it on another occasion.

In addition to meat for the grill, it is also important to consider side dishes. If you are having a large gathering, you may find it easier to purchase your side dishes pre-made. Pre-made side dishes, such as macaroni salads and fruit salads, are available for sale at most supermarkets. The only problem that you may find is that pre-made side dishes tend to be more expensive, when compared to preparing them yourself. Therefore, if you are looking to save money or if you only need a small amount of food, you may want to consider preparing your own side dishes.

As previously mentioned, many families have a backyard cookout or barbeque party; however, not everyone does, especially all of the time. Whether you and your family are just interested in playing outside for a short period of time or you aren't in the mood to cook a large meal, it may still be a good idea to have a collection of snacks on hand. On hand snacks are ideal during the summertime, especially for those who are actively participating in a number of outdoor activities.

Dry snacks are ideal for a number of different backyard activities. Most dry snacks are easy to eat on the go and they rarely ever leave a mess. The only downside to serving dry snacks is most snacks are unhealthy. If you are looking for tasty, but healthy snacks, you may want to examine foods that are low in sugar or low in fat. These items may include, but should not be limited to, fruits, vegetables, sugar free cookies, or low salt chips. Despite what you or your family may believe, many of these healthy snacks are just as good as those that are filled with unhealthy sugar.

One important thing that you must consider, whether you are barbequing or just having an outdoor snack, is water. Water is important, especially during the summertime. Water, unlike many caffeinated beverages and sugary drinks, is a great way to stay hydrated. Unfortunately, without water many children and adults become dehydrated. Dehydration is a dangerous problem. That is why it is important to have water and other beverages on hand. In addition to traditional water, you or your family may also enjoy the taste of flavored water. For many, flavored water is a healthy, but tasty alternative to traditional drinking water.

 By keeping the above mentioned points and suggestions in mind, you and your family are sure to have a fun backyard experience, accompanied by refreshing drinks, great food, or tasty snacks. Whatever the occasion calls for, there are a number of different foods that can help make your next backyard outing one of the best.

Popular Backyard Activities for Adults

When most of us think of backyard activities, children come to mind. While children may enjoy being outside, they are not the only individuals who enjoy participating in backyard activities. In fact, many adults also enjoy being outside in their yards. Whether you are retreating your backyard alone or with some friends, you may want to think of some fun or relaxing backyard activities. This can easily be done by examining some of the most popular backyard activities, especially those that are designed with adults in mind.

As previously mentioned, many adults use their backyards to relax. If you are looking to do this, you may want to examine your backyard or patio furniture. The furniture that you have available may make it possible, or even impossible, to enjoy a relaxing afternoon in your yard. Popular furniture, used to help achieve relaxation, may include lounge chairs or hammocks. If you do not have any comfortable lawn or patio furniture, you may want to consider purchasing some. Most, on and offline retail stores, carry a fairly large selection of patio furniture.

Although many adults use their backyards as a source of relaxation, others use it for excitement. If you are looking for fun backyard activities, there are literally an unlimited number of things that you can do. These activities may include playing sports games, going for a swim, or having a barbeque. All of these backyard activities are ideal for individuals of all ages, especially adults.

If you are interested in playing sports games in your backyard, you will have to think about the games that you would be interested in playing. You may also want to examine whether or not you would be playing alone or with someone else. If you are interested in playing a game by yourself, basketball or a singles game of horseshoes may be ideal. In addition to being ideal for singles games, horseshoes and basketball are also great games for when more than one player is participating. Additional multiplayer games may include soccer, football, tennis, badminton, or volleyball.

The above mentioned games are ideal because just about everyone one can participate in them. Most backyards are able to accompany a number of different backyard sports games. However, to go swimming, you will have to have a pool. Even though pools are popular, not everyone has one. If you are unable to have an in-ground or an aboveground pool installed in your backyard, a kiddy pool maybe a nice alternative. While kiddy pools are designed with small children in mind, they are great for wading in hot weather, even for adults.

A barbeque is another backyard activity that is enjoyed by many adults. Since most households already have a grill, you may not have to purchase anything besides your food. If you do not have a barbeque grill, many small ones can be purchased for around twenty dollars. Barbeques are great backyard activities, all on their own, but they also work well in conjunction with swimming or other outdoor activities.

In addition to enjoying, the above mentioned, popular backyard activities for adults, you may also want to make up your own. Whether you create your own unique game or stick to traditional backyard games, it is likely that you will be pleased with your decision to entertain yourself outside. There are many adults that just enjoy being outside, even if they are not participating in anything particular.

Popular Backyard Activities For The Whole Family

When summer arrives, the use of a backyard increases. This is due to the fact that most individuals do not like staying inside when the weather is so beautiful. If you are one of those individuals, it is likely that you and your family will be spending a fairly large amount of time outside. To make your time memorable and enjoyable, you may want to consider familiarizing yourself with popular backyard activities, especially those that are designed with the whole family in mind.

One activity that everyone enjoys is eating. Whether it be breakfast, lunch, or dinner, you may want to consider having your next meal outside. If you have a barbeque grill, you and your family may enjoy having tasty food that was prepared on the grill. If you do not have a grill, but are interested in purchasing one, you have a number of options. A large number of retail stores, both on and offline, carry a fairly large selection of barbeque grills. Charcoal grills are a cheap way to cook; many can sell for as low as twenty or thirty dollars.

In addition to having a backyard barbeque, your family may also enjoy a backyard picnic. Backyard picnics are often easier to prepare than most barbequed meals. If you wish, you could easily prepare all of your food inside. Popular picnic foods may include, but should not be limited to, sandwiches, subs, coleslaw, salads, crackers, cookies, and pretzels. If the weather is warm, you may also want to make sure that you include extra water. Water, especially during hot weather, is important for hydration.

While eating outdoors is a great way to spend time in your backyard, it will only take a few hours. If you are interested in spending the whole day in your backyard, you will want to find other backyard activities. One of those activities is likely to include swimming. Swimming is a favorite summer pastime, for individuals of all ages. The only downside to swimming is that you must have a swimming pool. If you do not have a swimming pool and cannot afford to purchase one, do not worry. There are literally an unlimited number of other backyard activities that your whole family could enjoy, even without a pool.

Other popular backyard activities involve the playing of sports games or water games. Water games, like many other backyard games, are ideal for individuals of all ages. To cool off or just participate in a family fun activity, you can purchase a water sprinkler, water balloons, or water guns. Many of these items can be purchased for an affordable price at most, on and offline, retailers.

If sports are more your family's style, you may want to examine purchasing a volleyball net or a basketball hoop. While a basketball hoop or a volleyball net may be an expensive purchase, it is likely that you and your children will enjoy them on more than one occasion. If you are concerned with the cost of a basketball hoop, volleyball net, or other sports equipment, you can purchase cheaper alternatives. Other popular sports games, which do not require the purchase of expensive equipment, may include kickball or softball.

Spending the day in your backyard is a great to not only have fun, but to spend quality time with your family. A backyard campout may be the perfect end to the perfect day. Camping is enjoyed by many. Backyard camping is great, especially if you have small children. Not only may they enjoy the new experience, but you will also be close to you home if something goes wrong. For a reasonable price, if you don't already have one, you should be able to purchase a tent and other camping supplies.

As you can see, there are a large number of backyard activities that your whole family may be able to enjoy. In fact, the above mentioned activities are just a few of the many that are available. For additional activities, you may want to ask the rest of your family for suggestions. It is possible that they may alert you to a fun backyard activity that you never even heard of before.

Own a Pool? Have a Pool Party

Every summer, millions of homeowners think about having a backyard party. Unfortunately, many are unsure about what they should center their party on. If you are looking to plan a party, you do not have to limit yourself to a traditional barbeque. If you have a swimming pool, you may want to think about hosting a pool party.

Pool parties are the perfect way to get friends, families, neighbors, and coworkers together, especially during the summer months. One of the many reasons why you should consider having a pool party is because it is likely that your party will stand apart from the rest. Most households in America have a barbeque grill; however, not everyone has a pool. The pool alone, may make your backyard party better than most.

One of the reasons why a pool party is a great idea, especially during the summertime, is because of the heat. In many areas of the United States, it is too hot to do many outdoor activities, especially without a way to cool off. Therefore, in addition to spending quality time with your friends, family, neighbors, or coworkers, you may also be providing them with a fun way to stay cool. This is nice because, as previously mentioned, not everyone has the luxury of owning a pool.

Another reason why you may want to host a pool party is because pools are fun, for individuals of all ages. This means whether you are inviting adults, children, or both, everyone should be able to enjoy your pool. Despite the fact that even children enjoy swimming, they may need more attention than adult swimmers. If children will be attending your pool party, you may want to develop a safety plan, just in case. This safety plan may include when children can swim or who will be watching over them when they do.

While a pool party is enough to bring in excited guests, you may also want to incorporate other backyard activities. One backyard activity that you may want to think about including is a barbeque. A swim party with a barbeque would literally be the ultimate backyard party. Not only will your guests have the opportunity to cool off in your pool, but they would also get to eat amazing food. If you are planning on having a large number of guests, you may want to think about asking others to help you prepare food. In most cases, your guests would be more willing to bring a small side dish or drinks.

To please your pool party guests, especially those that are looking for entertainment, you may also want to have some sports equipment on hand. In addition to traditional backyard sports games, such as football, basketball, or horseshoes, you may want to include water games. These games may include, but should not be limited to, water basketball or water volleyball. If you do not already have a basketball hoop or volleyball net, for your pool, you should easily be able to purchase either one form most online retailers or from your local pool supply store.

Whether you have just a pool party or a pool party with additional backyard activities, your party is sure to be a success. Whatever food, snacks, drinks, or activities you have on hand, your guests will likely be pleased with the fact that they can enjoy an afternoon away from home.

Planning A Pool Party: What You Need To Prepare For

Each year, a large number of Americans search for the perfect party idea. If you have a pool in your backyard, you may already have what is needed for the perfect party, a pool. Pool parties are nice because they not only allow you to socialize with those that you know, but they also give everyone a way to cool off. If you are thinking about hosting a pool party, you will need to start planning. Despite what you may think there is actually a lot of planning involved in hosting a pool party.

Perhaps, the first step in planning a pool party is to let everyone know that you are having one. Although pool parties may not be like birthday parties or Christmas parties, you may still want to send invitations to your guests. These invitations, if you choose to send them, do not have to be elaborate. In fact, since your pool party will most likely be casual, your invitations should be as well. If invitations are not your style, you will want to phone your friends or send them an email, inviting them to your pool party.

Once you have let your guests know that you are planning a pool party, you can then start preparing for the party. While it is not always important, you may want to consider confirming with guests whether or not they will be able to attend. Having an accurate guest count may help you better prepare for your party. In fact, a guest count may enable you to determine how much food, drinks, or snacks you should have on hand.

If you are planning on including a barbeque with your pool party, you will need to decide what type of food you would like to serve. Like any other special occasion, you may want to have a wide variety of different foods. This will ensure that there will be at least one thing on the menu that each guest will enjoy. In addition to main courses, such as meat, you will also want to include side dishes. These side dishes commonly include fruits, vegetables, and salads.

After you have decided which foods you would like served at your barbeque, you will also need to think about making them. Even if your party isn't for a few weeks, you may still want to develop a cooking schedule ahead of time. Although your main courses, such as barbequed meat, will be prepared the day of your pool party, you may want to prepare everything else earlier that day or the day before. This will help not only to ensure that you get all of the food prepared on time, but that you are also able to enjoy your own party.

As previously mentioned, you may want to include a barbeque with your pool party; however, it is not required. If you are planning on having a pool party, without serving a large meal, you may still want to have snacks and drinks on hand. Non-alcoholic drinks and most snack foods can be purchased for a reasonable price. Alcoholic drinks make for a great party, but some drinks can be expensive to purchase, especially in large quantities.

Aside from the food and entertainment, you may also want to make sure that you have a number of pool supplies and accessories on hand. These items may include, but should not be limited to, beach balls, lifejackets, arm floaters, swim rings, floating chairs, and other popular swim toys. If you do not already have a large collection of swim toys, you can easily purchase a few low-cost ones. Many pool toys, such as swim rings, arm floaters, and beach balls, can be purchased for a reasonable price. In fact, many of these items only cost around two or three dollars. It may also be a good idea to have extra towels on hand, just in case any of your guests forget to bring theirs.

Although pool parties are designed to be fun, you may want to establish some pool rules ahead of time. These rules may help to keep your pool and your pool party guests safe, especially young children. Whether you plan a simple pool party or an elaborate one, it is likely that you will be happy with your decision to plan your party, ahead of time.

Popular Water Activities For The Backyard

Each summer, millions of families head outdoors. Many times, they head to their own backyards. While being outdoors is nice, it can also be hot. In many areas of the United States, the temperature rises to beyond comfortable, especially during the summertime. Hot weather does not mean that you and your family should stay inside; however, you may want to think about backyard activities that can help you stay cool. You will find that many of these activities are centered on water.

Perhaps, one the best ways to stay cool in the summertime is to go for a swim. Many families own a swimming pool. If you do, it is a great way for you and your family to have fun. Despite the fact that many families have a pool, not all do. If you do not have a swimming pool, you may want to think about purchasing one. While most in-ground and aboveground pools are expensive, there are a few cheaper alternatives. These alternatives may include inflatable aboveground pools or kiddy pools. Most of these pools can be purchased for a reasonable price.

If you are unable to have a pool, even an inexpensive one, you do not have to worry. There are still a number of other fun backyard water activities that you and your family can enjoy. One of those activities may include a water gun fight. Water gun fights are a great way to cool off, but they are also a lot of fun. Individuals of all ages, include adults, small children, and teens, love playing with water guns. If you don't already own water guns, you should be able to purchase them for a reasonable price. They should be available for purchase at a number of popular retail stores.

In addition to water guns, water balloons are another fun backyard water activity. Large or small water balloon packages can be purchased from most retail stores, including dollar stores. Water balloons are great for individuals of all ages; both adults and children seem to enjoy them. Similar to water guns, water balloons are a fun, exciting, and competitive backyard activity.

Competitive and interactive water games are great for excitement; they are not right for everyone. If you are looking for a more civilized way to cool off, you may want to consider purchasing a water sprinkler. A water sprinkler, once connected to a hose, will spray water. Depending on the water sprinkler you purchase, water will often spray in a number of different directions. While water sprinklers are ideal for all households, they are great for those that are without a pool or limited on space.

To participate in many of the above mentioned water activities, such as water balloon fights or water gun fights, you may want to have access to a garden hose. Most water guns and water balloons can be filled up with a kitchen sink; however, it may convenient to use a water hose. Not only will a water hose make it easier to keep on playing, it may also help to keep your house clean and dry. With an outdoor water hose, there is no reason why anyone should be entering your home with, potentially messy, water toys.

Whether you make the decision to participate in one of above mentioned backyard water activities or all of them, you are almost always guaranteed a good time. Cooling off in the summer and playing with your friends or family, what could be better than that?

Planning A Backyard Barbeque Party

If you regularly cook your meals on a barbeque grill, you are not alone. Grilling is a popular American pastime. While many individuals end up grilling for their family, not everyone makes the decision to host a backyard barbeque party, despite the fact that it is a good idea. If you are interested in socializing and sharing good food with your friends, family, coworkers, or neighbors, you may want to, at least, think about planning a backyard barbeque party.

Backyard barbeque parties, like most other parties, require planning. While the planning associated with a backyard barbeque may not be as large as most other parties, it is still important. The proper planning of a party, including a barbeque, will help to ensure that your party is the best that it can be. For that reason, you may want to start making party plans as soon as you make the decision to host a party.

Since backyard barbeque parties are centered on food, you will want to think about the food that you will serve. To please all of your party guests, you will want to have a fairly large selection of meats. This will help to make sure that all of your party guests are able to eat the foods that they like. In addition to meats, you may also want to think about side dishes. Popular barbeque party side dishes may include, but should not be limited to, toss salads, macaroni salads, coleslaw, and fruit salads.

In addition to the foods that you are interested in serving, you may also want to plan how those foods will be made. Of course, the purpose of a barbeque party is to grill the foods then, but most of the side dishes will need to be prepared ahead of time. To ensure that all of your side dishes are prepared on time, you may want to start cooking them the day before your barbeque or earlier that morning. If you are having a large party, you may need to make a large amount of food. If this is the cases, it may be a good idea to have party guests bring a small side dish.

Aside from the main food, served at your barbecue, you may also want to think about drinks and snacks. For a reasonable price, you should be able to obtain a number of different snacks for your barbeque. Great snack ideas include crackers and cheese, cookies, chips, and pretzels. For drinks, you need to decide as to whether or not you want alcoholic beverages served at your party. Regardless of whether or not you choose to serve alcohol, you should be able to purchase your party drinks from most supermarkets.

While backyard barbeques are center on food, additional activities may be a good idea. At most department stores, you should be able to find a number of affordable toys or backyard activities. Many individuals, especially teens or adult males, enjoy playing sports. A football, basketball or horseshoe pit may be a great addition to your backyard barbeque. If children will be attending your party, you may want to have child friendly games on hand.

If you have a pool, it may be a good idea to incorporate swimming into your backyard barbeque; however, it is optional. If you are planning on allowing your party guests to use your pool, you may want to think about establishing some rules. These rules should focus on pool safety and children in the pool. While establishing rules at your barbeque may seem like a bad idea, it is not, especially when it comes to pool safety.

Of course, you will also want to invite your guests to your party. This can be done with formal invitations, a quick phone call, or a quick email. In addition to informing guest of your impending barbeque party, a guest list may also help you prepare for the big day.

The Benefits Of Organizing A Backyard Barbeque

Each year, a large number of Americans cook a barbequed meal in their backyard. Despite the fact that barbequing is a popular backyard activity, there are many individuals that never think about having a backyard barbeque party. If you love entertaining guests and barbequing, you may want to think about making your next party a barbeque party.

Perhaps, one of the greatest benefits to having a backyard barbeque party is that you will have a chance to see everyone that you know. When planning a backyard barbeque, many party hosts make the decision to invite their friends, family, neighbors, and sometimes even coworkers. Whether you get to see these individuals on a regular basis or on a rare occasion, you may enjoy having all of your friends and family together in one place.

In addition to inviting those that you know, a backyard barbeque party can give you the opportunity to familiarize yourself with new friends or family members. Whether your family recently grew, through marriage or birth, or a new neighbor moved into the area, you may want to consider hosting a backyard barbeque. Not only will a backyard barbeque give you the opportunity to meet new people, it may also make those new people feel welcomed.

Oh course, perhaps, the greatest benefit of hosting a backyard barbeque party is that you will have a chance to relax. Despite the fact that you may be the party host, you will likely find that you are able to find time to enjoy your own party. This can easily be done by taking small breaks or by seeking assistance from others. Whether you invite your friends, family, neighbors, or coworkers, it is likely that a number of your party guests would be more than willing to help you set up lawn furniture, cook food, or even clean up.

Another one of the many benefits to planning a backyard barbeque party is that you can plan your party anyway that you want it. This means that if you are only interested in having a small gathering, you can do so. You can also decide which food, drinks, or snacks are available to guests. You can also determine when your party will start and when it will end. This freedom is ideal because it can prevent you from stressing too much over planning the perfect party.

The good thing about backyard barbeque parties is that most can be planned in a short period of time. While it is still advised that you plan certain things ahead of time, such food, drinks, and party games, you do not necessarily have to. With a little bit of hard work and determination, you may be able to throw a backyard barbeque party together in a couple of days, or even in a few hours. The more assistance you are able to receive, the quicker you may be able to plan a party, including a backyard barbeque.

As you can easily see, there are a number of different benefits to hosting your own backyard barbeque. Whether you have a reason for planning a backyard barbeque party or not, it is likely that you will be glad that you decided to plan it. In fact, many party hosts find that they had so much fun that they end up hosting another party soon after.

Backyard Play Structures For Children

Playing outside is fun, but many children get bored with traditional outdoor activities. To cut down on the boredom in your family, you are encouraged to think about purchasing your child an outdoor play structure. Outdoor play structures are different than most toys because they are larger in size and often come equipped with more than one activity. If you are interested in purchasing one of these popular play structures, you may want to take the time to familiarize yourself with what is available.

When familiarizing yourself with popular outdoor play structures, you will find that you have a number of different options. Perhaps, the easiest way to go about seeing what is available is to visit your local retail stores. Many home improvement stores, toy stores, and department stores should have a fairly large selection of play structures available. In addition to seeing what is available locally, most storefront retail locations will have displays setup. These displays may give you an idea as to what your child's new toy will look like in your backyard.

While it is nice to view the selection of local play structures, you may also want to examine a number of different online retailers. You may not get to see product displays, but you should be provided with detailed information, including pictures. What is nice about online shopping is that most online retailers have a larger product selection, when compared to most traditional retail stores.

Whether you shop online or at one of your local retail stores, it is likely that you will come across a number of different items that are referred to as play structures. As previously mentioned, most play structures are large in size and are often equipped with more than one activity. Popular play structures include, but should not limited to, swing sets, playhouses, sandboxes, and tree forts.

Sandboxes are often referred to as outdoor play structures because they are made of durable materials. Popular sandbox styles include ones that are made with plastic or wood. It is also important to note that sandboxes come in a wide variety of different sizes. This means that if you have a large yard or a small yard, you should be able to find a sandbox that is perfect for your child.

Tree forts are another popular backyard play structure. Unlike many other play structures, tree forts may be hard to find for sale. This is because a large number of them aren't just big, but enormous. If you are able to find tree forts for sale, it is likely that only the supplies are for sale. It is rare to find a fully assembled tree fort in most, on and offline, retail stores. If your child would like to have a tree fort, but you are unable to find the supplies for sale or make one yourself, you may want to seek the assistance of a professional contractor.

Tree forts are many children's dream toy; however, not every child can have one. If you are unable to afford the cost of a tree house or if you do not have any trees in your backyard, you may want to think about purchasing a playhouse. In a way, playhouses are similar to tree forts. The only difference is that playhouses are ground structures. Playhouses, like most other outdoor structures, come in a wide variety of different styles. Many of these styles are great for boy, girls, or even both.

The above mentioned play structures are ideal for small children; however, if you are looking for a structure that can be used for a long period of time, even as your child grows, you may want to look into swing sets. Swing sets often come equipped with swings, slides, teeter totters, and monkey bars. Metal swing sets are available for a reasonable price. For a more expensive and dependable structure, wood swing sets are also available.

In addition to tree forts, playhouses, swing sets, and sandboxes, there are also a number of other outside play structures that are available for sale. Whether you purchase one of the ones mentioned above, another, or make your own, your child will likely be pleased with the purchase. So pleased, that they may never want to play inside again.

Building a Tree House or Fort: The Ultimate Backyard Experience

Each year, a large number of children play outside. Unfortunately, many of those children easily experience boredom. If you are the parent of one of those children, you may have searched high and low for the ultimate backyard experience. In your search, it is likely that you may have come across tree houses or forts. These structures offer most children an unlimited amount of fun. In fact, you may find that your child doesn't want to leave their newly constructed tree house or fort.

While tree forts or houses are fun to play in, there is something that is even more exciting than playing in them. The process of making and designing a tree house or fort is something that you and your child will likely never forget. Therefore, if your child does not already have a tree house or fort, you may want to consider making one. To get the most out of this experience, you will want to make it together.

To build a tree house or fort, you may need to have a tree. While a tree is a vital part of a tree house or a tree fort, it is not necessarily required. If you only have small, unstable trees in your backyard or none at all, you can still build your child a fun play fort or house. Instead of building the structure in a tree, you will just have to build it on the ground.

The first step in building or designing your own tree house or fort is to familiarize yourself with all of your options. When making your child a tree house or fort, you can design the structure a number of different ways. Despite this freedom, you are advised to examine popular tree house or fort designs and plans. In addition to giving you structural ideas, you may also be provided with detailed construction manuals.

Perhaps, the easiest way to familiarize yourself with tree house or fort designs is to use the internet. By performing a standard internet search, using the words tree house deigns, you should be provided with a number of different links. These links should take you to a website that offers tips, detailed directions, or ideas for building a tree house or fort. If you are able to find the tree house or fort of your child's dreams, you may want to print off all applicable information, including building guides or instruction manuals.

In addition to using the internet, to familiarize yourself with tree house or fort designs, you may also want to visit your local book store or library. There are a number of books and resources guides that are available. These resource guides, like the ones found online, should provide you with pictures and detailed directions. If your local book store or library does not have any tree house or fort books, you may want to search for books online.

Once you have found the tree house or fort that you would like to build, you will need to purchase building supplies. These supplies may include, but may not be limited to, wood, nails, screws, and other common tools. In most cases, you should be able to purchase the supplies that you need from your local hardware store. If your local hardware store does not carry all of the needed materials, you should be able to find them for sale online.

When it comes time to build your child's tree house or fort, you will want to keep them involved in the process. While they may be uninvolved in actual building process, there are other ways that you can use their assistance. After you have reviewed the construction directions, you may want to have your child read you the directions as you go along or hand you the materials that you need. No matter how large or small their part is, your child will likely be happy that you involved them in the process.

Exploring Nature With Your Child, In Your Own Backyard

Backyards, they are where individuals of all ages go to relax and have fun. While many people enjoy being in their backyards, they are not the only ones. In fact, when you are in your backyard, you are rarely ever alone. At any given time, your backyard is filled with amazing, living things. If you are the parent of a young child, you may want to use this opportunity to explore nature with them. Not only will it be a fun experience, but it will also be a learning experience.

Birds are just a few of the many animals that can be found in your backyard. There is a good chance that a large number of different birds will make their way into your yard, especially if you have a bird feeder. One of the many reasons why bird watching is fun is because of all the birds that you will see. In addition to just watching these birds, you may to document what your child sees.

To turn bird watching into an educational experience, you will need to purchase a few supplies. These supplies may include a bird watching book, a notebook, and a camera. Notebooks and cameras are optional; however, they are a great way to document the birds that enter your yard. While a notebook and a camera are optional, you may seriously want to consider purchasing a bird watching book. Many book stores carry a large selection of bird watching books, including those for children. A bird watching book is essential when incorporating education into this fun backyard activity.

As previously mentioned, birds are just a few of the many living creatures that can be found in your backyard. You and your child should also be able to find a large number of different bugs and insects. As with bird watching, you may want to study and examine some of these insects. By visiting your local book store or by shopping online, you should be able to find a number of insect resource guides or books that are designed especially for children.

What is nice about most bugs and insects is that you don't just have to look at them. A number of bugs and insects can live in small containers. If your child not only wants to see an insect up-close, but see how they go about their daily activities, they should be able to that with the right supplies. Most retail stores, including science stores, toy stores, and traditional department stores, should have a wide variety of different insect catching supplies. These supplies may include, but are not be limited to, small cages, breathable containers, and butterfly nets.

Many children are aware of the fact that bugs and birds are living animals, but many do not know that plants and flowers are also living. For that reason, you may want to teach them about plants and flowers. Depending on when your backyard was lasted mowed, you should be able to find a number of different plants and flowers. As with most other living things, you should also be able to purchase books and resource guides that cover common plants and flowers. You and your child may have fun comparing the plants and flowers in your backyard to those in their books.

It is amazing what you can find in your own backyard. While you may not give any thought to the plants, flowers, bugs, or birds that can be found in your backyard, your child will likely be impressed with them. For a fun, but educational experience, you and your child are encouraged to get outside and see everything that nature has to offer.

Download 100+ Books
Completely Free!
No Hassles...
No Charges...
Just Click And Download
100% Free!
CLICK HERE

This Product Is Brought To You By